The
Vietnam War

Douglas Willoughby

Heinemann
LIBRARY

H www.heinemann.co.uk
Visit our website to find out more information about Heinemann Library books.

To order:
☎ Phone 44 (0) 1865 888066
▤ Send a fax to 44 (0) 1865 314091
▢ Visit the Heinemann Bookshop at www.heinemann.co.uk to browse our catalogue and order online.

First published in Great Britain by Heinemann Library,
Halley Court, Jordan Hill, Oxford OX2 8EJ,
a division of Reed Educational and Professional Publishing Ltd.
Heinemann is a registered trademark of Reed Educational and Professional Publishing Ltd.

OXFORD MELBOURNE AUCKLAND
JOHANNESBURG BLANTYRE GABORONE
IBADAN PORTSMOUTH (NH) USA CHICAGO

Designed by AMR
Illustrated by Art Construction and Chris Brown (Pennant Illustration Agency)
Originated by Dot Gradations
Printed by Wing King Tong in Hong Kong.

ISBN 0431 11985 6
05 04 03 02 01
10 9 8 7 6 5 4 3 2 1

British Library Cataloguing in Publication Data to follow
Willoughby, Douglas
   The Vietnam War. – (20th century perspectives)
   1.Vietnamese Conflict, 1961–1975 – Juvenile literature
   I.Title
   959.7'043

Acknowledgements
The publishers would like to thank the following for permission to reproduce photographs:
Associated Press, pp. 30, 31; Bettmann/Corbis, pp. 36, 37; Corbis, pp.13, 15, 27, 43; Corbis/Peter Turnley, p. 39; Corbis/Wally McNamamee, p. 42; Corbis/Bettman, pp. 5, 6, 8, 21; Corbis/Everett, p.41; Corbis/Tim Page, p.17; Hulton Getty, pp. 7, 9, 11, 12, 14, 18, 19, 20, 22, 28, 32, 34, 35, 43; Katz, pp. 24, 25; Magnum/Marc Ribould, p. 27; Network, p. 38, Peter Newark, p.33; Rex Features, p.40.

Cover photograph reproduced with permission of Corbis.

Our thanks to Christopher Gibb for his comments in the preparation of this book.

Every effort has been made to contact copyright holders of any material reproduced in this book. Any omissions will be rectified in subsequent printings if notice is given to the publishers.

Words appearing in the text in bold, **like this**, are explained in the glossary.

Contents

The Vietnam War – an overview

Today, Vietnam is a united country. It is about 1600 kilometres long and covers an area of approximately 300,000 square kilometres, so it is a bit bigger than Italy. To the north is China, with Laos and Cambodia to the west. The South China Sea lies to the east. Over seventy-seven million people live in Vietnam, many along the Red River in the north, or in the delta of the River Mekong in the south. Some live in large cities like the capital, Hanoi, or Ho Chi Minh City (formerly Saigon). Many more are peasants, farming land that has been cleared from the tropical forests. Between May and September, the monsoon rains fall and the water is harnessed to grow rice, the main crop and the basic diet of the people. Along the coastal area, fishing and shipping are important sources of employment, but farming remains the main occupation.

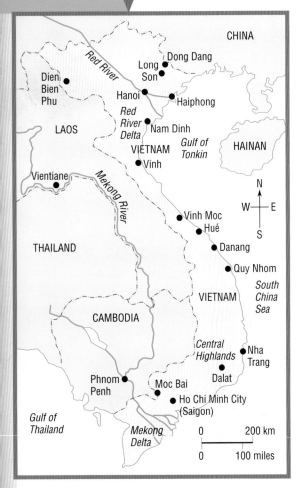

Map of modern Vietnam.

One of the longest wars in modern history

Vietnam has not always been a united country. In 1954, it was divided between north and south. From 1962 until 1975 it was the scene of one of the longest wars in modern history, the Vietnam War. This war was a **civil war** between **communist** North Vietnam supported by China and the Soviet Union, and 'free' South Vietnam backed mainly by the United States. During the thirteen years of the conflict, about 2.8 million American soldiers found themselves fighting a North Vietnamese Army (**NVA**) and a communist guerrilla army (the **Vietcong**) in the jungles of Vietnam. More than 58,000 of them were killed and 304,000 were wounded. The Americans were joined in the war by around 50,000 Australians, of whom 500 were killed, and a small group of New Zealanders, of whom 39 lost their lives. Sixty-eight American women were killed in the fighting, many of them nurses, aid workers and missionaries.

Vietnamese suffering

The Americans, Australians and New Zealanders and their communist enemy, the North Vietnamese Army and the Vietcong, who fought in the war, all suffered tragic losses of life. The main sufferers, however, were the ordinary people of Vietnam. In the three years beginning in

February 1965, the Americans dropped a million tonnes of bombs on North Vietnam. They followed this with a programme of chemical warfare. They also used deadly **napalm**, which killed many civilians. By the time the war ended, many of their farms were destroyed, their land polluted by chemicals and as many as a million Vietnamese, for a variety of reasons, had become **refugees**.

US soldiers burning a Vietnamese village.

The war and the media

The Vietnam War was the first war to be intensively covered by television cameras as well as by newspaper reporters. Modern technology meant that people throughout the world could see as well as read about the war almost as it was being fought. For many Americans, seeing their young men fighting, suffering and dying in the Vietnamese jungles was a shocking experience. Support for the war, which had been so strong at the beginning, changed to opposition. Enthusiasm turned to hostility. Many joined protest movements demanding an end to the war and the return of the thousands of young Americans fighting in it. Above all, the American public began to ask questions such as 'What are we doing there?' and 'How did we get involved?'.

The end at last

On 29 March 1973 the last American troops left Vietnam. Many who survived the conflict are still suffering both the physical and psychological effects of their shocking experiences in the war. On 30 April 1975, the communist North Vietnamese Army and the Vietcong army marched into Saigon, the capital of the south and occupied it. Soon afterwards, Vietnam was united once again but this time under communist rule. For those Americans who had fought in Vietnam, news of the fall of Saigon must have been particularly painful and many must have asked 'What was the point of it all?' 'For what purpose did so many of us die?' Although in recent years those who fought and died in Vietnam have been given fitting memorials, those same questions continue to be asked and the answers still remain painful to hear.

The background

From 111 BC until independence in AD 938, Vietnam was part of the Chinese empire. This long period of Chinese rule left its mark on the Vietnamese language, its religion. and the appearance of its buildings. The Vietnamese were strongly Buddhist. In the 17th century, French Christian missionaries arrived. At first they received a friendly welcome, but this changed to hostility when they began converting the people to the Catholic religion. This became so disruptive that, in 1857, French troops were sent in to protect the Catholic community. This was the first time that the French government became involved in Vietnam and it gave them an excuse to expand their overseas empire. Hostility continued. In 1858, the French Emperor, Napoleon III, sent 14 ships and 2500 troops to the port of Tourane (now Danang). Fighting continued until 1868 when the Vietnamese emperor surrendered and made a peace treaty with France. In 1885, the Chinese signed an agreement accepting French control over Vietnam. In 1893, the French added Laos and Cambodia to their empire which, together with Vietnam, became known as French Indo-China.

In 1858, Emperor Napoleon III of France sent troops to Vietnam to establish French control.

A French colony

Vietnam had valuable natural resources. By the turn of the century, the French were taking advantage of everything that her new colony had to offer – large amounts of coal, tin, zinc and rubber were being sent to France and Vietnam was becoming a market for French manufactured goods. By 1938, 57 per cent of all Vietnam's imports were produced by French firms. To exploit these benefits fully, the French increased their control over the country. They built a system of roads, canals and railways to transport raw materials and finished goods.

When it came to governing the colony, the highest officials were French, but at the middle and lower levels, the French made use of the Vietnamese. Many of these had become Catholics and had learnt to speak French in French schools. Some of these pro-French Vietnamese became rich and powerful, but for the peasants and ordinary Vietnamese life remained hard. The people paid taxes to the French to meet the cost of developing the country. Those who were unable to pay these taxes had to sell their land and work in the mines or on the rubber plantations. The protests that followed were put down by force. Some of the protest leaders decided to leave the country rather than risk death. One of these was Ho Chi Minh, who was to become the leader of the movement for Vietnamese independence.

Ho Chi Minh and Vietnamese communism

Ho Chi Minh, also known as Nguyen Ai Quoc (Nguyen the Patriot), was born in 1890 and died in 1969. His father lost his job as a teacher when he refused to learn French. He spent his time helping the peasants, for example, by writing letters for them, and brought his family up to believe in the importance of resisting the French. Ho's sister received a sentence of life imprisonment for stealing weapons from the French whilst working for them. Ho attended a grammar school and became a schoolteacher. Shortly afterwards, he left Vietnam. By 1914, Ho was working in the kitchens of a London hotel and in 1917 he arrived in Paris, where he studied the writings of Karl Marx and became a communist. He helped to found the French Communist Party in December,1920, and in 1925 set up the Revolutionary Youth League of Vietnam, followed by the Vietnamese Communist Party in 1930, and the League for the independence of Vietnam in 1941.

Ho Chi Minh 1890–1969, communist leader of the North Vietnamese.

Communism – the answer to Vietnam's problems

Perhaps Ho's most important experience came in 1924 when he visited the Soviet Union. The country was becoming **communist** after the 1917 revolution and Ho was very impressed by what he saw. He believed that communism was the answer to the problems of poverty facing the Vietnamese peasants. The land, owned by a few rich landowners, must be taken from them and given to the peasants. For this to be achieved, there would have to be a violent revolution. The French would be thrown out and the communists would take control of the country. If this was to happen, the peasants must be organized and trained. This was the job of the Communist Party which he would lead. For Ho, communism and Vietnamese freedom went together. However, he knew that if he returned to Vietnam he would be imprisoned. So he settled in China, close to the Vietnam border. Here he set up the 'Vietnam Revolutionary League', which, he hoped, would eventually lead the revolution.

The Japanese invade

In September 1940, as part of their plan for territorial expansion, the Japanese invaded Vietnam. The French surrendered and Ho saw the opportunity he had been waiting for. He returned to Vietnam in February 1941 and formed an army – the **Vietminh**. Led by General Giap, they began a **guerrilla war** in the jungle against the Japanese, using weapons supplied by the Soviet Union and by the United States, who declared war on Japan in December 1941. In August 1945, following the dropping of atomic bombs on Japan by the USA, the Japanese surrendered and Ho thought that Vietnam was now free. After all, the French had gone and the Japanese had been defeated, albeit with American, French, British and Russian help. Surely the independence of the Vietnamese would be recognized.

In September 1945, therefore, he announced the creation of the Democratic Republic of Vietnam. This was what he had dreamed of and worked for over many years. After the war ended until 1946, Vietnam was occupied by China and Britain. Ho believed that it was only a matter of time before they handed over power to him.

When the new Vietnamese Republic was set up in 1976, Giap became Vice Premier.

General Giap

Vo Nguyen Giap was born in 1912. As a student, he became a communist and joined Ho Chi Minh's Reolutionary Youth League of Vietnam in 1926. In 1939, Giap fled to China to avoid arrest by the French, but his sister-in-law was executed and his wife died in a French prison. Giap was Ho's assistant in the guerrilla war against the Japanese (1941–5). He commanded the Vietminh against the French between 1946 and 1954. The victory at Dien Bien Phu was his greatest triumph. He remained Commander-in-Chief of the Vietminh throughout the Vietnam War until 1975. When the new Vietnamese Republic was set up in 1976, Giap became Vice-Premier.

The French return

Ho was therefore angry when, in 1946, Vietnam was returned to the French, who refused to accept the Democratic Republic of Vietnam. Ho and the Vietminh now found themselves fighting yet another war, this time against the French. After early setbacks, the Vietminh began to win important victories, particularly after 1949, when the Chinese **communists** helped them. But, in 1953, victory seemed

French paratroopers watching comrades being dropped over Dien Bien Phu in 1954. The French were defeated after a 56-day siege.

a long way off. The French still controlled the south, supporting Bao Dai, the former emperor, as head of state. Ho realized, however, that the longer the war lasted, the greater were the chances of a Vietnamese victory. He also knew that in France, the people were tired of the fighting. Ninety thousand French troops had already been wounded or killed in a war lasting seven years. There was no sign of victory and the cost of the war was a great burden on French taxpayers. With declining support the French desperately needed to end the war with a victory. Their commander in Vietnam, General Navarre, hoped to achieve this in 1954 at Dien Bien Phu.

The Battle of Dien Bien Phu

To stop the Vietminh forces returning to their bases in Laos, Navarre set up a defensive system at Dien Bien Phu (see map on page 10). He knew that to reopen the route into Laos, the Vietminh would have to attack it. Instead, led by Giap, they surrounded it with thousands of troops and a vast system of well-constructed trenches. They maintained their siege for 56 days, during which time the attention of the whole world was focused on that French garrison and on what would happen to the besieged soldiers. For all those 56 days, they were subjected to a constant bombardment from siege guns placed in the hills over the French camp. On 7 May 1954, the siege came to an end. Around 2000 French troops had been killed and over 10,000 surrendered. Vietnamese losses were between 8000 and 10,000 and bodies of soldiers from both sides remain buried in the defensive system, even today. The French suffered a humiliating defeat which meant the end of their control of Vietnam and Indo-China. For Ho Chi Minh and for General Giap and the Vietminh, Dien Bien Phu was a great victory and would now surely lead to a united, free and communist Vietnam – at least, that is what Ho and his followers believed was about to happen.

America gets involved

In April 1954, shortly before the French surrender at Dien Bien Phu, the foreign ministers of North and South Vietnam, Cambodia, Laos, China, the United States, the Soviet Union, Britain and France met in Geneva, Switzerland to try to reach a peaceful solution to the problems of Korea and French Indo-China. The Geneva Accords, as they were known, were of great importance. They set the scene for the Vietnam War and speeded up American involvement.

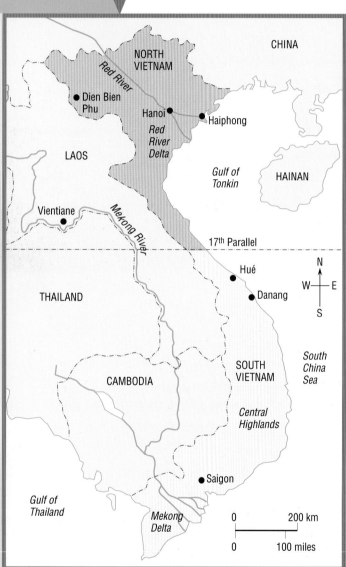

Map of Vietnam after the Geneva Accords.

The Geneva Accords

- There was to be a cease-fire
- Vietnam would be divided at the 17th parallel of latitude.
- North Vietnam would be **communist** and ruled by Ho Chi Minh.
- South Vietnam would be ruled by Ngo Dinh Diem, a strong opponent of communism.
- French troops would leave Vietnam.
- The **Vietminh** would leave South Vietnam. Each side had 300 days to withdraw troops.
- The Vietnamese people could choose to live in the north or the south.
- By July 1956, a general election would be held throughout Vietnam for the people to decide the future of the country.

Although some of his supporters were angry that Vietnam was still not a united communist country after the defeat of the French, Ho Chi Minh was not worried. He knew that in the free elections the communists would win. Most of the Vietnamese were poor peasants who believed that their lives could only be improved if the communists took power and gave them land. In the USA, President Eisenhower had reached the same conclusion and suggested that if free elections were to be held, as many as 80 per cent of the Vietnamese would vote communist. He therefore decided that the USA must make sure that those elections never took place.

The Cold War begins

After World War Two, the United States
and the Soviet Union became the world's
great superpowers, joined after the
revolution in 1949 by communist China.
The Soviet Union was communist and the
United States **capitalist**. Neither trusted
the other. Each believed the other
country was trying to destroy it and the
other countries it influenced. So, after
1945, the **Cold War** began. The
Americans saw the Soviet Union as an evil
threat which must be resisted. Speaking to
Congress as early as March 1947, President
Harry Truman had set out, in what became
known as the Truman Doctrine, what the
United States should do to stop
communism spreading. The Americans must
help any country fighting communism by
sending them money and weapons and, if
necessary, soldiers to fight with them.

Harry S. Truman, President of the USA, 1945–1953. He believed the US should help any country fighting communism.

Closely connected to the Truman Doctrine was the **domino theory**,
which stated that if communism took over one particular country then
those nearest to it were immediately at risk and likely to fall next. A
look at the map of Indo-China will show clearly that this area was a
perfect example of the domino theory in action. The Americans
believed that, if Vietnam fell to communism, then Laos, Cambodia and
Thailand would immediately be threatened.

Eisenhower

Eisenhower became President in 1953. He continued Truman's policy. In
the early years of his presidency, however, Eisenhower moved slowly. He
realized that the American people would not support sending troops to
Vietnam, particularly since more than 50,000 US soldiers had recently
been killed fighting in Korea. Instead, he sent in a small group of
'advisers' under Colonel Edward Lansdale, whose task was to use
advertising, propaganda and American dollars to persuade the South
Vietnamese people not to support the communists in the forthcoming
elections. Instead, they should vote for Ngo Dinh Diem as president –
the man backed by the Americans.

America gets sucked in

Ngo Dinh Diem

Ngo Dinh Diem, President of South Vietnam from 1955 until his assassination in 1963.

Unlike the majority of Vietnamese, Ngo Dinh Diem was a Catholic, his ancestors having been converted by French missionaries in the 17th century. He was educated by the French, worked for them as an administrator and at the age of 25 became a provincial governor. Dinh Diem spent some of the French Indo-China War, between 1946 and 1954, in the United States meeting influential Americans and convincing them that he should be a future leader of the South. So effective were his efforts that the USA nominated him as South Vietnamese president at Geneva in 1954. If the Americans backed Dinh Diem because they thought they could control him, they were mistaken. He often ignored their advice – but they kept up their support because there was no alternative.

In October, 1955, Dinh Diem was elected president of South Vietnam in elections which were violent and hardly fair. Shortly afterwards, he made a grave error. Having received a reminder from the North that under the Geneva Agreement, a general election for the whole of Vietnam was due in July 1956, he refused to accept the elections. As many as 100,000 people from a variety of political and religious groups protested, and then were imprisoned or killed. The Americans now found themselves supporting a president who was becoming increasingly unpopular with the people in a situation where violence was escalating.

NLF founded

Throughout Vietnam, **communist** supporters of Ho Chi Minh and many others were horrified at the refusal of Dinh Diem to hold a general election. Some resorted to a violent terror campaign and in 1959, 1200 government officials were murdered. Ho disliked this approach, and in 1960 brought all the different groups together as the 'National Front for the Liberation of South Vietnam', the **NLF**, or '**Vietcong**' as the Americans called it. Their aim was to remove the Diem government by any means, including violence, and replace it with a government representing all the people of Vietnam. Just as important was their promise to the peasants that they would give them land. This promise made it certain that, from now on, most of the peasants would support the Vietcong in the war which was about to begin. Thus, in 1960, the battle lines were being drawn up. The NLF or Vietcong, with Chinese and, if necessary, Russian support, were preparing to fight a war against the Diem government in the south, backed by the Americans.

President J. F. Kennedy and Vietnam

John F. Kennedy, who was elected US president in 1960, was a strong believer in the Truman Doctrine and the **domino theory**. According to him, the USA would be willing to *'pay any price, bear any burden, meet any hardship, support any friend, oppose any foe to assure the survival and success of liberty'*.

Consequently, Kennedy was happy to continue American involvement in Vietnam and to increase it if victory was a possibility. In 1961, he sent money to the South Vietnamese to increase their army from 150,000 to 170,000 soldiers, plus another 100 advisers to train them. This decision was kept from the American public because it broke the Geneva Agreement.

Inauguration of John F. Kennedy as president of the USA, 1961. Kennedy was assassinated in 1963.

John Fitzgerald Kennedy (1917–1963) was born in Brookline, Massachusetts. He was the second son of Joseph Kennedy (1888–1969), a rich banker and financier who served as American ambassador to London between 1938 and 1940. John was educated at Choate School, Harvard University and the London School of Economics. During World War Two, he served as commander of a torpedo-boat in the Solomon Islands and was badly wounded. He entered politics when the war ended and sat as a Democratic Congressman from 1946. In 1952, he was elected senator for Massachusetts.

In January 1961, he became the first Roman Catholic president in America's history and at the age of 43, the youngest. He began his presidency with high ideals and the promise of a 'new frontier' for the American people – civil rights and a better life at home and more opportunities to serve underdeveloped countries abroad. In foreign affairs, he soon found himself with problems, particularly in 1962, when Soviet missiles were found in Cuba. He also increased US involvement in Vietnam. On 22 November 1963, in Dallas, he was assassinated.

The Vietcong and guerrilla warfare

Between 1963 and 1973, the Americans were in Vietnam, fighting a **guerrilla war** mainly against the **Vietcong**. The Vietcong fought in small groups and used their knowledge of their own countryside to hide from the Americans and to pick the places where they themselves wanted to fight.

Mao Tse Tung and guerrilla warfare

Mao Tse Tung had used guerrilla tactics when leading the **communist** revolution in China, which ended in victory in 1949. Ho Chi Minh and the **NLF** greatly admired Mao and decided to use the same tactics against the Americans and South Vietnamese army in Vietnam. They organized the guerrilla army into small groups of between three and ten soldiers, called cells. The cells worked together but had little knowledge of each other, so that if any were captured and tortured, they would not give away too much information.

Mao Tse Tung, Chairman of the Chinese Communist Party and president of the People's Republic of China, 1949–1976.

Peasant support

If the Vietcong guerrillas were going to win the war, they must have the support of the peasants. They needed food, shelter and somewhere to hide when being hunted. Mao, like Ho the leader of millions of peasants, believed that 'without the constant and active support of the peasants, failure is inevitable' and stressed the importance of treating them with respect. Ho's NLF guerrillas had to follow a strict code of conduct:

* Do not destroy the land and crops of the peasants, their houses and belongings.
* Do not force the peasants, against their wishes, to sell or lend you anything.
* You must always keep your word.
* Do not do or say anything which will lose the respect of the peasants.
* You must help the peasants in their daily work, e.g. collecting firewood.

Guerrilla tactics

The NLF won the support of the peasants because they promised to take land from large landowners and give it to the peasants. The NLF also told them that the Americans and South Vietnamese would take the land back, so the peasants agreed they would feed, shelter and hide the guerrillas in return for land. In some cases, they actually became guerrillas and joined the war. The vast majority of peasants backed the guerrillas but those who refused, despite the code of conduct, were often threatened and beaten.

Soldiers in the jungle crossing a monkey bridge built of bamboo and vines.

Using the peasant villages as their base, the guerrillas went out into the jungle. They attacked units of the South Vietnamese army, the **ARVN** (Army of the Republic of Vietnam), and ambushed patrols of American soldiers. They then disappeared back into the jungle. They hid in the villages in the houses or in tunnels built for the sole purpose of hiding them and linked directly to the jungle. When the Americans arrived, there was no sign of the enemy.

American soldiers often tortured the villagers to get information and sometimes burnt their houses and crops. This angered the peasants even more and made them support the NLF.

A US marine captain described the problem: *You never knew who was the enemy and who was the friend. They all looked alike. They all dressed alike. They were all Vietnamese. Some of them were Vietcong … . The enemy was all around you …*

Jungle tactics

Out in the jungle, the guerrillas never chose to fight unless they were certain of winning. They often attacked small enemy patrols, usually at night. Early in the war, they used simple daggers and swords. Later, they were able to use better weapons, including explosives captured from the Americans. The American soldiers suffered a terrible ordeal. The jungle they had to patrol was dense and the rice fields wet. The heat was often intense, the climate unfamiliar, and they were attacked by insects and leeches. There was also the threat of Vietcong booby traps, sharpened bamboo staves, mines, **grenades**, and artillery shells, waiting to be stepped on and set off. The guerrillas realized that the longer the war lasted, the greater were their chances of victory. They knew that the Americans would give in before they did. After all, this was the guerillas' home.

The Ho Chi Minh trail

For the **guerrilla war** to succeed, the **NLF** had to keep their guerrilla armies in the south equipped with fresh troops, supplies and weapons. Many of these supplies and weapons came from **communist** China and the Soviet Union and the fresh troops came from North Vietnam. They all arrived in the south along the Ho Chi Minh trail. This was a collection of paths and routeways through the jungle. **Vietcong** guerrillas travelled down the trail from the north to join the war in the south. The NLF received about 60 tonnes of supplies each day using the trail. They were carried by a variety of different methods, including lorries, oxen and bicycles. Along the trail, there were camps where the guerrillas could rest and receive medical treatment.

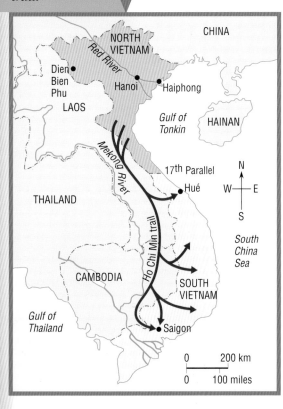

Map of Vietnam showing route of Ho Chi Minh trail.

When the war began, it took as long as six months to travel down the trail from North Vietnam to Saigon. As the war continued, the trail became wider through increased use. By 1970, the journey was being completed in six weeks. The Ho Chi Minh trail was so vital to keeping the guerrillas supplied that the Americans tried to bomb it, but the jungle was so thick that they found it difficult to see it from their planes. To stop the trail being used, the Americans did try to lay mines and barbed wire across it, but they abandoned this idea in 1967 when the Vietcong attacked the soldiers laying them. Electronic devices dropped to detect enemy movement were unsuccessful. They picked up everything that moved – including animals.

The Tet Offensive

The Vietcong spent most of their time fighting in the jungle, but at times they came out to attack the Americans directly. The Tet Offensive on 31 January 1968 was directed at targets throughout South Vietnam.

In September 1967 the NLF launched attacks on American garrisons. The Americans were pleased that, at last, the Vietcong appeared to have left the jungle and that, by the end of 1967, the Vietcong had lost 90,000 men. General Westmoreland, the commander of the US forces, was sure that with such heavy enemy losses, an American victory was now certain. But Westmoreland had been tricked. On 31 January 1968, during the Tet New Year festival, 70,000 North Vietnamese soldiers and Vietcong launched surprise attacks on 36 cities and towns throughout South Vietnam. It was now clear that the attacks on US garrisons the previous September, had been intended to draw American soldiers from the towns they were defending to prepare for the Tet Offensive.

The Americans were shocked by such well-organized attacks and by how easy it was for the NLF to attack so many towns and cities. What surprised them most was the way in which the Vietcong entered the grounds of the US Embassy in Saigon. They did not capture the building but killed five American marines and took the main radio station. The Americans were also deeply worried that the NLF were able to find 70,000 new soldiers so soon, having lost 90,000 up to the end of 1967.

From a military viewpoint, it could be said that the Tet Offensive was an American victory. The US lost 1536 soldiers with 7764 wounded, but 45,000 NLF soldiers were killed. What was most important, however, was that the American people and politicians now realized that they had been duped by Westmoreland and his military staff. Westmoreland had deliberately falsified reports to Lyndon Johnson, who became president in 1963 following Kennedy's assassination. The USA could not win the Vietnam War. The NLF had vast numbers of soldiers. Coming into South Vietnam down the Ho Chi Minh trail, they would eventually overwhelm the Americans.

A wounded woman is carried away from the shelling as **refugees** *flee Saigon after the Vietcong attack.*

Lyndon Baines Johnson (1908–1973) was born in Stonewall, Texas, in 1908. He began his working life as a teacher and was elected to the House of Representatives as a Democrat in 1937. During World War Two he served as a naval officer whilst still a congressman. He was elected a senator for Texas in 1948 and became US vice-president when Kennedy became president in 1961. Immediately after Kennedy's assassination in 1963, Johnson was sworn in as president and re-elected in 1964. At home, he introduced medical benefits for older people and civil rights laws. He became unpopular, however, because he escalated US involvement in Vietnam. As more and more American soldiers died, he became increasingly disliked. He decided not to seek re-election to the presidency in 1968. He retired to his Texas ranch where he died in 1973.

US strategies and tactics

Strategic hamlets (safe villages) policy

The Americans used a variety of methods to fight the **Vietcong** in the jungles of Vietnam. The strategic hamlets (safe villages) policy was introduced under President Kennedy from 1962. Its purpose was to isolate the Vietcong from the villages of South Vietnam and deprive

US soldiers with two villagers from a 'safe village'.

them of the supplies and soldiers they needed. This was done by moving the villagers away from the Vietcong and placing them in new villages surrounded by barbed wire and guns. By September 1962, about a quarter of the South Vietnamese population was said to have been moved into safe villages. The policy failed. The peasants hated being moved from the villages that they and their ancestors had lived in for years. They also hated having to leave their land and resented having to work building trenches to protect the villages. The policy became so unpopular that many peasants actually joined the Vietcong. The 'Hearts and Minds' campaign tried to win the Vietnamese peasants over by attempting to persuade them that the Americans were on their side. This policy also failed.

Search and destroy

In 1965, General Westmoreland began a more direct 'search and destroy' approach. Its purpose was simple – to find the Vietcong in the jungle and the villages and destroy them. US soldiers patrolled through the jungle and into the villages to find **guerrillas** – a more difficult task than it sounds. It was often impossible for the Americans to tell the difference between the guerrillas and the peasants. They often killed innocent civilians by mistake and sometimes deliberately. The war was now taking on a very racist quality. US soldiers called their opponents 'gooks' and had a tendency to shoot any they saw – it increased the 'body count'. Some collected enemy ears as souvenirs. The Vietcong responded by torturing US prisoners.

Around villages controlled by the Vietcong there were networks of tunnels in which the guerrillas could hide from the Americans.

They were built large enough for the guerrillas to hide in but too small for the Americans. Sometimes, in frustration, the Americans tortured Vietnamese villagers to find out where they were hiding the Vietcong. This angered the villagers, increasing their support for the **communists** and making sure that 'search and destroy' failed.

Bombing North Vietnam

In March 1965, under 'Operation Rolling Thunder', the Americans began the bombing of North Vietnam. Its aim was to destroy the economy of the north and stop the support for the guerrillas in the south. It was only intended that the bombing would last for eight weeks. In fact, it lasted eight years, during which time, 8 million bombs were dropped. This was over three times the number of bombs dropped in the whole of World War Two. The Americans may have taken care to ensure that only military targets were bombed but accidents were bound to occur and civilians were killed. The bombing of military and industrial targets in North Vietnam failed. North Vietnam was mainly a farming country, which did not have many military and industrial targets. Most important of all, the Chinese and Russians were able to replace all the military supplies and troops which American bombing destroyed.

NUMBERS OF US TROOPS IN VIETNAM, 1962–72	
YEAR	TOTAL
'ADVISERS'	
1962	12,000
1963	15,000
1964	23,310
GROUND TROOPS	
1965	184,310
1966	385,300
1967	485,600
1968	536,000
1969	484,330
1970	335,790
1971	158,120
1972	24,000

(SOURCE: STANTON'S VIETNAM ORDER OF BATTLE)

US bombers attacking North Vietnam in 'Operation Rolling Thunder'.

Ground troops

The **Gulf of Tonkin Resolution** in 1964 gave the president freedom to take action in Vietnam. The first US troops to arrive in Vietnam, apart from advisers, were 3500 marines who landed on 8 March 1965. For the next three years, the number increased rapidly, reaching 536,000 by 1968. President Johnson was determined to fight communism in Vietnam by sending in more and more troops. American troops stopped South Vietnam from collapsing but could not defeat the Vietcong, although in early 1968 Johnson and many of his generals still believed that they were winning.

Methods of warfare

The Americans in Vietnam were able to draw on a vast arsenal of different types of weapons and associated technology:

- Helicopters were widely used by the Americans. They were used to transport troops, quickly and at short notice. They were also used to remove soldiers from the jungle if the fighting became too difficult or if they were injured. Between 1965 and 1973, helicopters carried 406,022 injured US soldiers to hospitals. Whilst using helicopters may have had its benefits, it did mean that the Americans had even less direct contact with the peasants, essential to victory in such a **guerrilla war**.

- Throughout the war, the American Seventh Fleet, made up of 125 ships and 64,000 men, controlled the seas around Vietnam. From their aircraft carriers, they sent fighter planes and bombers to attack the North. From offshore, battleships shelled **Vietcong** positions. They also tried to stop supplies reaching the Vietcong from the sea by **blockading** the coast. Hundreds of ships were stopped and searched but there were so many that some supplies slipped through.

- The Americans fighting in Vietnam made considerable use of **anti-personnel bombs**. Pineapple bombs were made up of about 250 metal pellets inside a small canister. When they were dropped, thousands of pellets were thrown horizontally over the ground hitting everything and everybody around. Plastic and metal needles, rather than metal pellets, were sometimes used in anti-personnel bombs. The advantage was that plastic could not be detected on X-rays. Anti-personnel bombs injured rather than killed civilians. Injured people put greater pressure on hospitals and created more disruption.

US aircraft spraying defoliants on dense jungle growth.

- The great problem facing the Americans in Vietnam was actually finding the Vietcong in the thick, tropical jungle. For this reason, in 1962, President Kennedy approved 'Operation Ranch Hand'. This involved spraying chemicals from aircraft over the jungle to try and destroy the vegetation and reveal guerrilla hiding places. The chemical used was '**Agent Orange**', which contained traces of the most toxic forms of **dioxin**. In 1969, 1,034,300 hectares of forest were destroyed.

Not only did Agent Orange destroy thousands of trees but it was later found to have caused birth deformities in children. It also caused cancers in soldiers fighting in the war.

- Chemicals were also sprayed on all crops. Between 1966 and 1969, the chemical 'Agent Blue' was sprayed over 278,640 hectares. The aim was to deprive the guerrillas of food. In fact, the ordinary peasants suffered most from the poor rice harvests that followed the spraying. They also suffered because the land that they and their ancestors had farmed for generations was polluted by the chemicals and remained unworkable for many years. Between 1962 and 1971, the Americans sprayed about 72 million litres of **herbicide**, including more than 42 million litres of Agent Orange, on the jungles of Vietnam to destroy the Vietcong's cover. Many American soldiers claimed that the vegetation grew again very quickly and was thicker than before.

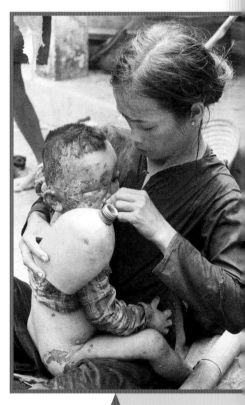

A Vietnamese mother gives water to her child, burnt by napalm.

- As well as dropping explosive bombs and chemicals on Vietnam, the Americans also used bombs containing chemicals that caught fire. Of those used, **napalm** is the best known. Napalm is a mixture of petrol and chemical thickener. It produces a tough sticky gel that attaches itself to the skin. The chemical within it, white phosphorus, goes on burning for a considerable time. Three-quarters of all napalm victims in Vietnam were burned through to the muscle and bone. The pain alone often caused death because it was so intense. Photographs of Vietnamese civilians, particularly children, burnt by napalm, were seen throughout the world and did much to damage the reputation of the Americans and their cause in Vietnam.

I have heard and read that napalm melts the flesh, and I thought that's nonsense, because I can put a roast in the oven and the fat will melt but the meat stays there. Well, I went and saw these children burned by napalm, and it's absolutely true. The chemical reaction of this napalm does melt the flesh, and the flesh runs right down their faces onto their chests and it sits there and grows there … These children can't turn their heads, they were so thick with flesh … And when gangrene sets in, they cut off their hands or fingers or their feet.

An American woman from New Jersey, herself a mother of six children, describing her visit to a hospital in South Vietnam where she saw children suffering the effects of napalm.

US soldiers and the Vietnam War

During the course of the war, about 2.8 million American soldiers served in Vietnam. At the beginning, they were professional soldiers who had chosen to join the army as their career. They were well trained and committed. By 1967 however, most of the soldiers had been **drafted** (called up). The average age of US soldiers in Vietnam was 19 and their tour of duty lasted twelve months. About 60 per cent of the soldiers were likely to fight or be shot at. The others were employed in supplying the needs of the fighting troops but could be fired on at any time by the **guerrillas**. The average US soldier had a 2 per cent chance of being killed and a 10 per cent chance of being seriously wounded, but for those involved in the fighting, the casualty rate was of course far higher. Of those killed in the fighting, 43 per cent died within the first three months. In total, about 58,000 American service men and women were killed.

The draft

The US army drafted young American men at the age of eighteen. To reduce the stress on them, they served for just a year, which, it was hoped, would keep up morale. In fact, the only aim for many was to survive until their year was ended. When the young soldiers arrived in Vietnam, they were very often sent into units to replace men who had been killed or wounded. Known as 'cherries', they were often not accepted by the others in the unit because their inexperience might result in mistakes that could lead to loss of life. Not all young American men were drafted. Those who were at college and university could have their draft delayed.

American troops on patrol in the dense forest areas of Vietnam. Streams such as this were often booby trapped, making this kind of area especially hazardous.

Experiences of fighting

American soldiers involved in the fighting often found themselves in small units patrolling the jungle in search of guerrillas. As well as being worried that they might be ambushed, they had to be on the look-out for booby traps such as sharpened bamboo stakes hidden under sticks and leaves and **trip-wire** across a jungle path, which might set off a **grenade**. They also had to be careful that they did not trigger off a 'Bouncing Betty' mine by standing on it and causing it to explode, injuring all around. The climate in the jungle was damp, hot and humid, and heat exhaustion was common. Although it became cooler in the evening, the soldiers then had to cope with **malarial** mosquitoes. They found it impossible to find the guerrillas in the thick tropical jungle and this made them even more frustrated.

Soldiers and officers

Because many soldiers were serving in Vietnam for only a year, it was difficult to make each platoon an effective fighting unit. By the time many soldiers had become trained and fairly experienced, it was time to return home. Many also realized that since they were in Vietnam for only a year, the main aim must be to endure the year and get home alive. Their officers were different. They were professional career soldiers who saw success in the war as the way to gain promotion. Sometimes, they were prepared to sustain heavy losses to achieve success.

This illustration shows three types of booby traps used by the **Vietcong** in Vietnam.

In one battle to capture 'Hamburger Hill' from the **NLF**, about 450 American soldiers out of 600 were killed or wounded. After holding the hill for a day, Lieutenant-Colonel Weldon Honeycutt, the officer in charge, ordered the men to withdraw. Many soldiers were so angry with what Honeycutt had done, and that so many lives had been lost to achieve nothing, that attempts were made to kill him. He survived, but this is a good example of the anger felt by so many. In fact, it has been admitted that between 1969 and 1971, there were 730 reported attempts at '**fragging**' – the killing of an officer by his own men, of which 83 were successful. It is also recognized that the actual figures are probably higher.

Declining morale

The morale of American soldiers was high at the beginning of the war. They were professionals who believed that they were fighting for the freedom of Vietnam. As the fighting continued, the deaths increased, and more ordinary people – particularly blacks – were **drafted** against their will. Morale began to decline. Many began to question what they were fighting for and whether they could actually win. Those directly involved in the fighting realized that the war was going badly and lost confidence in their officers. They tried to desert. Between 1966 and 1973, 503,000 American soldiers attempted to desert.

Drugs

As the morale of US fighting troops fell and the boredom of those not directly involved grew, drug-taking increased. Many drugs were easily available and could be purchased cheaply throughout South Vietnam. Marijuana was the most popular. The Americans smoked it in their base camps and during periods of leave away from the fighting. Cocaine and heroin were also used. The troops used **amphetamines** to keep themselves awake during night patrols. The problem was so bad that in 1971, 20,000 troops were treated for drug abuse. Drugs seriously reduced the efficiency of US soldiers, much to the delight of the **Vietcong**.

The Massacre at My Lai

On 16 March 1968, a platoon of American soldiers in 'Charlie Company' approached the small village of My Lai, just south of Khe San. The platoon had already suffered fairly heavy casualties from booby traps, snipers and mines and were becoming frustrated that they could not find the Vietcong. The villagers were suspected of hiding **guerrillas**, but when the Americans arrived, they could find no trace of them. Under the command of Lieutenant William Calley, the platoon committed the worst recorded atrocity of the war. Later investigations revealed that 347 men, women, children and babies had been murdered. Some of the women had been raped first. Other reports put the number of deaths at over 500.

Men, women and children of My Lai after the massacre.

Full details of the massacre were kept from the public. The official version was that 90 Vietcong fighters had been killed and one American soldier shot in the foot. In November 1969, the full story broke. Americans were horrified by news of the massacre and that the news had been concealed for eighteen months. Calley was put on trial for murder, found guilty and sentenced to life imprisonment. He served three and a half years before President Nixon pardoned him.

The My Lai massacre divided American public opinion. Many believed that the soldiers' actions were right because the villagers were hiding the Vietcong. Others were horrified. Some were angry that only Calley had been tried. Americans realized that their soldiers in Vietnam were under great stress and pressure and that at My Lai in March 1968, they had simply cracked. The massacre confirmed the feeling, growing since the Tet Offensive of 1967, that the Vietnam War was now a war which America could not win.

Survivors of the My Lai Massacre.

Personal accounts

Calley had a clear idea of what he had done.

The only crime that I have committed is in judgement of my values. Apparently, I valued my troops' lives more than I did that of the enemy.
Vietnam, Alan Pollock

A My Lai villager saw the massacre differently.

It's why I'm old before my time. I remember it all the time. I'm all alone and life is hard. Thinking about it has made me old ... I won't forgive as long as I live – think of the babies being killed, then ask me why I hate them.
Four Hours at My Lai, Yorkshire Television

Lieutenant Calley at his trial.

*My troops were being massacred in Vietnam by an enemy they could not see. The enemy was **communism**. When I came face to face with it, I had to put the lives of my own troops first.*
Vietnam War, Simpkin

The Vietnamese people and the war

As early as 1954, Ho Chi Minh and the **communists** knew that Vietnam could only become independent and reunited by force. Only war could remove the armies that were occupying the country and preventing reunification. In the 1960s, the enemies were the Americans. To begin with, the communists used local **Vietminh** and **Vietcong** soldiers in the South but later these were joined by soldiers from the North, who travelled down the Ho Chi Minh trail. Generally, the **guerrillas** really believed in the cause for which they were fighting. Their generals were prepared to accept heavy losses, knowing they could easily get fresh troops. The Americans knew all too well that, if large numbers of their troops died, the war would become very unpopular at home. The North Vietnamese were fighting for their own country and for them the war had a clear aim – victory and reunification.

The majority of the North Vietnamese people supported the war and their government. Support came also from the Soviet Union, which provided 8000 anti-aircraft guns and 200 anti-aircraft launching sites for the North Vietnamese. Whilst morale amongst the communists was far higher than among the Americans, the war was not easy for them either, and there were exceptions. One young Vietcong soldier writing to his girlfriend in 1971 said, *'This terrible war makes so many strange thoughts race through my head. I would like to jump up thousands of miles to get away from here, from killing. Before, I did not know what it was like to kill a man; now that I have seen it, I don't want to do it any more. But it is the duty of a soldier to die for his country, me for our fatherland, the enemy for his. There is no choice.'* (Vietnam 1939–75, Neil de Marco)

Diagram showing underground air raid tunnels built by the Vietcong.

Although soldiers may be fighting on different sides and for different causes, their feelings about war and killing are often the same.

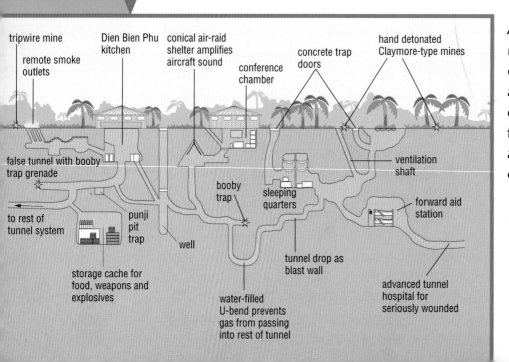

tripwire mine

remote smoke outlets

Dien Bien Phu kitchen

conical air-raid shelter amplifies aircraft sound

conference chamber

concrete trap doors

hand detonated Claymore-type mines

false tunnel with booby trap grenade

to rest of tunnel system

punji pit trap

well

booby trap

sleeping quarters

ventilation shaft

forward aid station

storage cache for food, weapons and explosives

water-filled U-bend prevents gas from passing into rest of tunnel

tunnel drop as blast wall

advanced tunnel hospital for seriously wounded

Bombs and shelters

What the people of both North and South Vietnam feared most was being bombed by the Americans. Between 1964 and the end of 1971, 6.2 million tonnes of bombs were dropped. This means 136 kilograms of bombs for every man, woman and child in Indo-China and 22 tonnes of bombs for every 259 hectares (square mile). In many areas, enormous craters covered the landscape and hundreds of villages were destroyed. Around a million Vietnamese civilians were killed and there were 5 million **refugees**. To protect themselves from falling bombs, the Vietnamese people built underground tunnels where they could shelter during attacks. The tunnels around Saigon stretched for 320 kilometres (200 miles) and were well planned and constructed. Others were built quickly without much planning and were not always reliable.

Vietnamese villagers carrying children, burned with napalm like Kim, away from a burning village.

Phan Thi Kim Phuc (Kim)

In 1972, Phan Thi Kim Phuc (Kim) was nine years old. The Americans had ordered the South Vietnamese air force to attack her village, Trang Bang, with bombs and **napalm** because Vietcong guerrillas were hiding there. With others, she sheltered in the pagoda. The pagoda was hit. Two of Kim's brothers were among those killed. The terrified survivors ran onto the road where an American photographer, Nick Ut, snapped them. The photograph became world-famous. It was named 'Vietnam's Most Harrowing Photo' and awarded the **Pulitzer Prize**. The photo shows the terror and horror of war, and how very often innocent people can be drawn into war and devastated by it. Kim survived the napalm attack. In 1996, she attended the annual Veterans Day Ceremony in Washington, DC and she is now a UNESCO Goodwill Ambassador. Her body still carries the scars left by the burns. She may have forgiven what happened but she will never be able to forget.

Photographer Vicki Goldberg was also at Trang Bang and later described what she saw:

The naked girl and the others ran toward us rather slowly, like people finishing their run. They passed the camera, it followed from behind. The girl's back and arm were seen to be completely covered with black patches of burned skin, no longer resembling flesh. American soldiers gave her a drink and poured water over her.

The anti-war movement

The protest movement against the Vietnam War, sometimes called the peace movement, began shortly after the war started. It lasted into the 1970s. At its height, millions were involved. The Vietnam war divided the American people. It also deeply divided the USA's European allies. It often resulted in great bitterness between those who supported it and those who opposed it. In the end, the protest movement was an important factor in the American decision to leave Vietnam and in ending the war itself.

Early protests

The first protest against US involvement in Vietnam took place in New York in 1963. It was organized by Thomas Cornell, a member of the Catholic Worker Movement. The following year, Cornell formed the Catholic Peace Fellowship with two priests, Daniel and Philip Berrigan. In 1964, a peace rally in Washington, DC was attended by 25,000 people. Some of those marching were socialists and **communists** who supported North Vietnam, but most were **pacifists**. They opposed the war because they believed that war and killing were morally wrong. Such a person was David Dellinger. He visited North Vietnam and saw for himself the suffering inflicted on civilians by American bombing, despite claims that only military and industrial targets were being hit. Pacifists were so sure that the war was wrong that in November 1965, one of them, a Quaker from Baltimore named Norman Morrison, set fire to himself in the street. A few weeks later two others followed him. This was done to gain publicity and to draw attention to their views.

The anti-war movement began with young people and students, but older people increasingly joined in. This is an anti-war rally in New York, 1967.

Students

Thousands of students across the USA became the most active protesters against the war. In 1965, more than 3000 attended the first anti-war 'teach-in' at the University of Michigan, sparking off 100 further teach-ins across the country. At these events, students refused to attend lectures and to leave their universities. Instead, they spent the time with their teachers discussing the war and their opposition to the USA's involvement in it. As this grew, student protests increased. In April 1965, 20,000 people attended a rally at the Washington Monument organized by Students for a Democratic Society. By 1967, student protests were becoming less peaceful. Strikes and shouting down government speakers were common.

The anti-draft movement

There were widespread protests against the **draft** by thousands of young Americans and their supporters. In 1965, David Miller publicly burnt his draft card and was sentenced to two and a half years in prison. In late 1966, there was an increase in anti-draft protests after Bruce Dancis, a student at Cornell University, destroyed his draft card and mailed the remains to his draft board. Cornell students formed the first 'We Won't Go' group, followed by two dozen such groups on college campuses. Burning draft cards became a common scene throughout the country, but the government was determined to punish those refusing to fight. When Philip Berrigan and three others poured blood on service records in the Baltimore Customs House, they were sentenced to six years in prison.

By the end of 1969, 34,000 draft dodgers were wanted by the police whilst between 1963 and 1973 9118 men were prosecuted for avoiding it. In all, around 40,000 young Americans left the country to avoid the draft, 30,000 going to Canada. What really brought home to Americans the horrors of Vietnam was the formation of 'Vietnam Veterans Against the War' in 1967. This was a group of ex-soldiers who had fought in Vietnam and who were campaigning for the end of the USA's involvement. They were given great publicity, particularly those disabled from injuries received in the fighting. They had seen the war at first hand and were now completely opposed to it.

Flowers were adapted as symbols of peace and love by the 'hippie' culture of the 1960s. Here a demonstrator offers a flower to American soldiers at an anti–war demonstration in Washington DC, 1967.

Martin Luther King

In April 1967, around 400,000 attended a mass protest in New York against the war, and 175 young men burnt their **draft** cards. Present at the demonstration was the great black civil rights campaigner, Martin Luther King. King attacked the war, not only because he thought it was morally wrong, but also because the money spent on it – $66 million a day – meant that Johnson had had to cut back his programmes to tackle poverty, especially among blacks. Most of all, King objected to the number of blacks fighting in Vietnam, when other young Americans, mostly white, at college or university, could defer the draft. Blacks formed a larger percentage of the US army in Vietnam than they did in the US population. Black militants wanted to go much further than King. They threatened to kill the whites who drafted them. In May 1967, the famous boxer, Muhammed Ali, was indicted for refusing to be drafted.

The march on the Pentagon

In 1967, 100,000 anti-war protesters gathered at the Lincoln Memorial in Washington. When the rally ended, over 50,000 people, led by the radical Jerry Rubin, marched to the **Pentagon**, the headquarters of the US military, to continue their protest. The Pentagon was surrounded by 10,000 troops, armed with tear gas, truncheons and unloaded guns. When the protesters attempted to enter the building, violence broke out and there were 1000 arrests. 1967 ended with opposition to the war increasing and becoming more violent.

Black civil rights leader, Martin Luther King, attacked the Vietnam war.

1968 – a terrible year for America

In the spring and early summer, Martin Luther King and Robert Kennedy, brother of the former president, were assassinated. Although the killings were unconnected to the war, they were seen as terrible signs of increasing violence. The Tet Offensive in January 1968 surprised the US military and made many realize the war could not be won. In a survey taken just after the Tet Offensive, 63 per cent of Americans opposed the war. Protests against the war continued in America and throughout the world. Most capital cities in Western Europe saw violent demonstrations, particularly London and Paris. There were similar scenes in Australia. Soldiers from that country were fighting in Vietnam and there was strong opposition to their involvement. In the United States itself, the government decided to crack down heavily on protesters, particularly those encouraging young Americans to avoid the draft. Dr Benjamin Spock, a famous expert on bringing up children, was indicted for draft-dodging. However, there were also parades supporting the war, often organized by World War Two veterans' organizations.

Rioting occurred at the 1968 Democratic Convention when the police and anti-war protesters clashed.

Johnson decides to stand down

On 31 March 1968, worn down by the growing opposition to the war, Lyndon Johnson announced that he would not be standing again for the US presidency. Robert McNamara, the US Defense Secretary, also announced his decision to retire. The anti-war movement saw the Democrat senator Eugene McCarthy as the man to follow Johnson. In Chicago in August, the Democratic Party would meet to select their candidate to stand for the presidency against the Republican, Richard Nixon.

Chicago 1968 – the Democratic Party Convention

About 5000 peace campaigners assembled in Chicago at the time of the Convention to protest against the war and to support McCarthy. Chicago's Mayor, Richard Daley, was ready for any troublemakers. A total of 26,000 police, soldiers and National Guardsmen had been assembled to protect the Convention. On Wednesday afternoon, when vice-president Hubert Humphrey was to be nominated as Democratic candidate, there were riots in Grant Park. Most protesters remained peaceful. Then they made their way to the Hilton Hotel, where the Convention was taking place. They were met by the police and many were tear-gassed and clubbed. The beatings were filmed by TV cameras and broadcast throughout the USA. Opinion polls later showed that most Americans supported the police action, including many who opposed the war. Seven protesters were later tried for conspiracy to incite (start) a riot. Five were found guilty but their sentences were overturned after they appealed against the verdict.

Nixon and continuing protest

In January 1969, Richard Nixon was sworn in as US president, promising to achieve in Vietnam 'peace with honour'. He wished to see an end to the war and troops coming home – but not just yet. Negotiations might be taking place in Geneva to end the war but the Americans would stay in Vietnam until the South Vietnamese were able to fight the **Vietcong** themselves. Protests against the war continued. Huge marches took place in 1969 and 1970. In April 1971, around 500,000 people led by 'Vietnam Veterans Against the War' took part in a protest in Washington. Two weeks later, only 15,000 took part in a demonstration in favour of the war. Whilst Nixon seemed to be promising an eventual end to the fighting, the war appeared to be escalating. In March 1969, he ordered the secret bombing of Cambodia – although this was totally against international law – because the Vietcong were using it as a base to attack South Vietnam. Yet in June he announced the first withdrawals of US troops.

In 1970, four students were killed during a demonstration at Kent State University, Ohio.

Kent State University – May 1970

In April 1970, Nixon announced that American troops had entered Cambodia to destroy **communist** bases used by the Vietcong. Protests took place in universities throughout the USA. On 4 May at Kent State University in Ohio, National Guardsmen opened fire on protesting students, killing 4 and injuring 9. The whole country was shocked by what had happened. The killings sparked off 400 protests and strikes in universities across the country.

Revelations about the 'Phoenix Program'

In 1971, information was released about the work of the Central Intelligence Agency (**CIA**) in the Vietnam War. In 1967, they set up the 'Phoenix Program'. Its purpose was to identify and arrest Vietcong suspects in areas controlled by the South Vietnamese. The target was 3000 suspects each month. The aim was to arrest them, get them to give information and then put them in prison. Between 1968 and 1972, 28,000 Vietcong suspects were captured and imprisoned. Another

20,000 were assassinated and 17,000 changed sides. The programme was effective and many communist bases were wiped out, but the methods were very controversial.

> *It was explained to us that anything alive in that area was supposed to be dead. We were told that if we saw a 'gook' (slang for Vietnamese) or thought we saw one, no matter how big or small, shoot first. No need for permission to fire. It was just an open 'turkey shoot' … men, women and children, no matter what their ages, all went into the body count. This operation went on for a few weeks. This was a regular 'search and destroy' mission in which we destroyed everything we found.*
>
> Sergeant James Weekes described orders he was given in May 1967. (*Vietnam 1939–75*, Neil de Marco)
>
> Evidence such as this increased the feeling among many Americans that the war was wrong and should be ended quickly.

Anti-war poster. 'Uncle Sam' had been used to recruit soldiers when the United States entered World War One in 1917.

Daniel Ellsberg and the Pentagon Papers

Daniel Ellsberg was a government employee who worked at the **Pentagon**. In 1967, he was asked to collect together all documents relating to Vietnam since 1940. There were 4000 pages. Ellsberg and others added another 3000 pages of analysis. Together, they became known as the 'Pentagon Papers'. The documents showed that government officials had often lied about or covered up incidents in the war. Ellsberg, who had become an opponent of the war, photocopied the documents and released them to the *New York Times*. They began to be published in 1971. Nixon attempted to stop publication and to prosecute Ellsberg for theft and conspiracy. The Supreme Court ruled that the publication of the papers was not illegal and all charges against Ellsberg were dropped. The papers revealed a great deal about what had happened in Vietnam which had been kept secret from the American people. It damaged the reputation of many involved in the war and strengthened the demands for peace.

Nixon: Vietnamization and peace

Richard Milhous Nixon (1913–1994)

Richard Nixon's family were Quakers. They ran a citrus farm. He graduated in law at Duke University, North Carolina. In 1942, during World War Two, he became a naval officer. When the war ended, he entered politics as a Republican, sat in Congress between 1946 and 1950 and then served as a senator until 1952. Between 1953 and 1961, Nixon was with Eisenhower's vice-president. Nixon supported America's **Cold War** stand against **communism**. In 1960, Nixon stood for election as President against the Democrat John F. Kennedy, but was defeated. He withdrew from national politics, returning in 1968 as Republican candidate for president. He narrowly defeated the Democrat Hubert Humphrey. Nixon set out to end the Vietnam war and improve relations with the communists. In 1972, he visited Beijing in February and Moscow in May. In 1972, Nixon was re-elected with a massive majority. His second term as president was dominated by scandals, of which Watergate was the most important. On 9 August 1974, he became the first ever US president to be forced to resign. He died in 1994.

Nixon was elected President in 1968 mainly because he promised to 'de-Americanize' the war. American troops would slowly be brought home, but the war would go on until 'peace with honour' had been won. For this, a policy of 'Vietnamization' would be followed. The soldiers of the South Vietnamese army would have to fight. The Americans would train and equip them but eventually pull out. Most important of all, the US Air Force would continue to support South Vietnam and would bomb the North and other targets, if necessary.

Peace talks

In May 1968, peace talks between the US and North Vietnam began in Paris. After one year, no progress had been made. The North Vietnamese wanted the whole of Vietnam to be reunited but the Americans wanted North and South to remain separate. North Vietnam wanted the communist **NLF** to be part of the new government in the south but the Americans wanted North Vietnamese and American troops to leave South Vietnam, followed by free elections. Nixon believed that bombing the North would make them accept peace. He was wrong.

A peace agreement

By October 1972, a peace agreement had been worked out between the USA and North Vietnam, four and a half years after negotiations had begun. The chief North Vietnamese negotiator was Le Duc Tho. Henry Kissinger represented the US. The terms of the peace agreement were:

- All fighting throughout Indo-China would stop.
- American troops would withdraw from Vietnam within 60 days of the end of the fighting.
- American prisoners of war, about 700, would be freed.
- Elections would be held in the South to choose a new government.
- Each side would stay only in those areas it controlled when the fighting stopped.

Henry Kissinger US Secretary of State, 1973–76. Kissinger was awarded the Nobel Peace prize in 1973 for his efforts to end the Vietnam War.

Nguyen Van Thieu, the South Vietnamese President, was furious at these terms. He realized that South Vietnam would be at the mercy of the North. But Kissinger was anxious for an agreement to be signed. The US presidential elections were due in November. If the war could finally be ended, Nixon was certain to win the election. When Van Thieu rejected the agreement, North Vietnam broke off negotiations. On 18 December 1972, Nixon ordered another massive bombing of the North. The North started negotiations again and Van Thieu was forced to accept the agreement. It was signed in Paris on 27 January 1973.

The Americans withdraw

In April 1969, the number of US troops in Vietnam was 484,330. In June, Nixon announced the withdrawal of 25,000 troops and a further 35,000 in September. By the end of 1971, only 158,000 remained. At the end of March 1973, the remaining 691 American prisoners in North Vietnamese hands had been handed back. The last American troops left Saigon on 29 March 1973. For the Americans, the Vietnam War was over, but not for the South Vietnamese.

The collapse of South Vietnam

In early 1973, as the Americans were leaving, South Vietnam appeared to be in a strong position. It had the world's fourth largest air force and an army of one million soldiers equipped with modern American weapons. The government of South Vietnam controlled 75 per cent of the country and 85 per cent of the people. The **communists**, on the other hand, were in a weak position. They were short of men, weapons, ammunition and food. During 1973, the southern forces had the better of the fighting on the border with Cambodia, with the North Vietnamese and **Vietcong** forces struggling to avoid defeat. The situation changed dramatically, however, and the army of South Vietnam soon began to collapse. By summer 1974, 90 per cent of South Vietnamese soldiers were not being paid enough to support their families. Government officials were stealing their pay and the soldiers were threatening the peasants for money.

The fall of Saigon

When the North Vietnamese and Vietcong forces moved further south, the South Vietnamese could not stop them. By late spring 1975, Saigon was surrounded. Van Thieu complained that the Americans had let the South down, yet it still had plenty of guns and tanks. What it lacked was organization and leadership. On 25 April 1975, Van Thieu fled South Vietnam with hundreds of government officials. They were all frightened that when the communists took over, they would be captured, tortured or even killed.

Nguyen Van Thieu became president of South Vietnam in 1967.

American troops leaving Saigon in March 1973.

On 30 April, the last 6000 Americans to leave Vietnam were lifted out by helicopter. Thousands of Vietnamese civilians who had worked for the Americans also wanted to leave. They too were frightened about what would happen to them when the communists arrived. Unfortunately, there was not enough room left on any transport leaving Saigon.

Panic set in as people fought for what places remained. On the same day, North Vietnamese and Vietcong soldiers entered Saigon. A tank broke down the gates of the presidential palace. The communists marched in. For all the people of Vietnam, the war was over.

The death toll

During the course of the war, about 2.5 million men, women and children were killed. Of these 900,000 were North Vietnamese and Vietcong soldiers, 223,000 were troops from South Vietnam, and about a million were civilians, many simply caught up in the fighting by accident. American military losses were 58,000, together with Australians and New Zealanders. The people of Vietnam and those of the USA were now about to start counting the cost in a variety of other ways.

Vietnamese suffering

Of the millions who were harmed or damaged by the Vietnam War, it was the ordinary Vietnamese who suffered most. According to Ha Van Lau, a **communist** officer, there was 'at least one dead, or some wounded in each Vietnamese family'. It is estimated that in 1975, in South Vietnam alone, there were 1 million widows. Around 800,000 children had been orphaned or abandoned, many of them by American soldier fathers.

Damage and destruction

Heavy bombing of both North and South left widespread damage and destruction. Buildings, roads, railways and bridges were destroyed and would have to be repaired before life could return to normal. The use of **herbicides** such as '**Agent Orange**' laid waste large areas of forests and crops. Sixty per cent of rubber plantations, 60,000 hectares of **mangrove** forests and millions of hectares of farm land were destroyed. Thousands of farm animals had been killed. Virtually all stocks of oil and petrol had been wiped out as a result of the bombing. Because so much farmland had been destroyed, many Vietnamese faced starvation and disease.

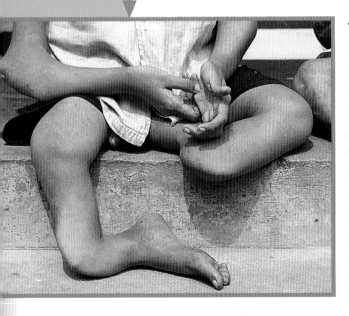

A Vietnamese child deformed by Agent Orange.

When the Americans left Vietnam, they left behind large amounts of weapons, including unexploded bombs and booby traps. These could kill civilians who might not know what they were. Herbicides and chemicals had long-term effects. After the war, many who had been exposed to them began to develop cancers. Their children suffered birth deformities. Even today, thousands of deformed children are growing up in Vietnam as a result of such chemicals as 'Agent Orange'. Babies have been born without eyes, with twisted limbs and even without brains.

Reconstruction

Immediately the war ended, Vietnam became a united country under the communists. A huge task of reconstruction began. The country was desperately short of raw materials and the wreckage of tanks and aeroplanes was used to rebuild factories and schools. All land was taken over by the state and farmers had to work on **collective farms**. The new communist government took over more than 500 factories in the South, producing textiles, chemicals, paper and foods. Heavy industry, such as iron and steel, was given priority. But there was no money to spend on rebuilding industry in the badly-damaged country. Reconstruction had to depend on gifts and loans from other countries. More than 100 nations including Sweden, Australia and the Soviet Union, which had broken off relations with Vietnam during the war restored them. All these countries provided money to help the rebuilding. The United States did not restore relations with Vietnam and provided no money. Vietnam remained a very poor country for many years to come.

Re-education

Vietnam was now a communist country, and a programme of **re-education** began. About 200,000 senior military officers and soldiers from South Vietnam were placed in camps where they worked all day and in the evenings were given instruction in communist theory and obedience to the government. Objectors were sent to the 'discipline house' where they were chained for many months, not permitted to see daylight and threatened with starvation. Many died, and by 1983 there were still 63,000 in prison.

Refugees

As in most wars, after the fighting stopped **refugees** became a serious problem. So much of the farming land had been destroyed that many left the countryside for the towns, especially Saigon, now renamed Ho Chi Minh City. Many in the North were attracted to what appeared to be a better lifestyle there. Attempts were made to close down bars and stop the drug trade. In 1975, about 230,000 South Vietnamese left the country to settle in the USA and Canada. This number increased in 1978 after the Vietnamese government introduced laws against the Chinese residents. Thousands of Chinese and Vietnamese refugees left Vietnam in crowded ships. Photographs of the 'boat people' left a lasting impression throughout the world.

'Boat people' from Vietnam set sail in tiny leaky boats to try and find a better life elsewhere.

The Americans and the Vietnam War

For millions of Americans, whether they were directly or indirectly involved, the Vietnam War was a terrible experience. It lasted for twelve long years and was the first major war in US history which the Americans lost. When the war finally came to an end in 1975, Americans began to count the cost in all sorts of different ways.

The financial cost

The Vietnam War cost the USA over 120 billion dollars. Even for the richest country in the world, this was a large amount. Most important of all, it meant that schemes to tackle America's social problems had to be postponed. Plans to clear city slums, to provide medical care for the poor and to reduce racial inequality could not be carried out, simply because the money was needed to pay for the cost of the war in Vietnam. Abandoning these plans caused considerable bitterness and anger in America. Many questioned whether the war was really necessary.

The US did not intervene when Soviet troops invaded Afghanistan in 1979.

The Vietnam Syndrome

As well as the financial cost, the USA paid a heavy price in human suffering in Vietnam. The war left many Americans dead or injured. As a result, many began to question whether the USA should continue to get involved in fighting in other countries even if it was for 'freedom and democracy'. The Truman Doctrine seemed to be replaced by the Nixon Doctrine, which appeared to state that American troops should only be sent into a country if the USA was directly threatened. This change in policy was a direct result of experiences in Vietnam – the Vietnam Syndrome. When Soviet troops invaded Afghanistan in 1979, the Americans did little or nothing to stop them. By 1991, however, this approach seemed to have changed again when the USA went to war against Iraq, after Iraq invaded Kuwait.

When one returning American soldier entered an airport bar, he was asked,
'*How do you feel about killing all those innocent people?*'
When he later offered to buy those in the bar a drink, he was bluntly told,
'*We don't accept drinks from killers.*'
(*Vietnam 1939–75*, Neil de Marco)

> Bruce was trained for undercover work in Vietnam. He spent a lot of his time killing people. He grew to like it and to love guns.
>
> *When I first got back I spent time in prison in California. I killed a man right here in the United States … . I do not trust anyone now. I would rather trust a dog than a person. A person is a vicious animal. I'm not a normal person by any means. A normal person can handle society. I can't. I do not like people … . I'll be pleased when it's done. When death comes, I think I'll welcome it.*

From the film Born on the Fourth of July, disabled war veterans protesting about poor medical treatment.

Experiences of veterans

American soldiers paid a heavy price for their involvement in Vietnam. Many who returned home when the war ended wondered what they had been fighting for. They had gone to Vietnam to support the South in the fight against **communism**. They had returned defeated, and angry that over 58,000 of their friends and comrades had been killed and over 153,000 injured. Nothing had been gained. Those who fought in Vietnam and survived expected a warm welcome when they returned. They were often bitterly disappointed. Some were even treated by fellow Americans as criminals and murderers. Medical treatment for the wounded and disabled was not always of a good standard and they found it hard to get jobs, despite laws giving them priority. The **Returned and Services League** did not always provide much assistance in finding work. Veterans who found it difficult to settle down again into civilian life felt betrayed by the country they had fought for. Those who had fought in Vietnam clearly had a different view of the war from many members of the American public. A public opinion poll taken in 1990 showed that 57 per cent of Americans thought that it had been wrong to get involved in Vietnam but 58 per cent of veterans thought it had been right.

Many soldiers who fought in Vietnam suffered not only physical injury but psychological damage as well. They experienced 'post-traumatic stress disorder', as a result of fighting in the jungle and seeing their fellow soldiers killed. As many as 700,000 veterans may have suffered from this condition. To many it brought depression and attacks of rage. Some found their marriages ending in divorce, others turned to drugs and alcohol. Suicides among ex-soldiers increased.

Changing public opinion

In most wars, public attitudes towards the fighting change dramatically during its course. This was certainly true of America during the Vietnam conflict. When the war began, most Americans supported it. The feature film *The Green Berets* was made during the early years of the conflict. The US army controlled the script and it starred John Wayne. The message of the film was clear. The Americans were wholly good, fighting for freedom and democracy. The **Vietcong** were wholly bad, fighting to destroy freedom and spread **communism**. This message seemed in tune with the thinking of the American people at that time. As the war continued, there was a change in public opinion. As more US soldiers were killed, opposition to the war grew. Films such as *Platoon* (1986), *Full Metal Jacket* (1987) and *Hamburger Hill* (1987) gave a more honest view. So brutally realistic and depressing were some of the scenes in *Platoon* that its director Oliver Stone had difficulty in finding a studio to make it. By the time the film *Born on the Fourth of July* (1989) appeared, highlighting the life of disabled veteran, Ron Kovic, the public had accepted more of the truth about the war.

The Veterans' War Memorial

In November 1982, the veterans who fought in Vietnam were finally given a national memorial in Washington. Why did it take so long for a memorial to appear? The answer is complex. Perhaps the American people were not ready to honour those who had died so soon after the war ended. Perhaps there was still a strong sense of guilt about what had happened in Vietnam and a lot of blame was still attached to those who fought there.

On 13 November 1982, 150,000 people assembled in Washington to witness the unveiling of the memorial to those who had died in Vietnam. It was the biggest crowd to assemble there since the funeral of John F. Kennedy. The veterans marched down

Granite wall showing the names of all American soldiers killed in Vietnam. Vietnam Memorial, Washington, DC.

Constitution Avenue to the memorial, which had been paid for out of private donations. Listed on it were the names of 58,132 men and eight women who died in the fighting. Also recorded are the names of 2413 others, Missing in Action. Important people made speeches, the crowd sang, 'God Bless America' and the memorial was dedicated. Thousands strained to touch the names of the dead.

Joel Swerdlow, a newspaper reporter later wrote: *'All afternoon, all night, the next day and the next and the next for an unbroken stream of months and years, millions of Americans have come and experienced that frozen moment. The names have power, a life, all of their own. Even on the coldest days, sunlight makes them warm to the touch … Perhaps by touching, people renew their faith in love and in life, or perhaps they better understand sacrifice and sorrow. We're with you, they say. We will never forget."*

Veterans marching in the ANZAC day parade in Adelaide, Australia.

In Australia Vietnam veterans led the march to remember ANZAC Day in 1987, and in October of the same year, a 'Welcome Home March' was held in the federal capital, Canberra. In 1992, in Canberra, the Prime Minister, Paul Keating, unveiled The Australian Vietnam Forces National Memorial. In both Australia and the United States, the two national war memorials commemorated those who had died in one of the worst 20th-century conflicts since the end of World War Two. Those who survived had finally seen their dead comrades remembered in a proper and dignified way. They could now try and get on with the rest of their lives.

Vietnam timeline

1868 Vietnam becomes part of the French empire.

1890 Birth of Ho Chi Minh.

1930 Ho Chi Minh helps to form Communist Party in Indo-China.

1940 Japan takes over Indo-China.

1941 Ho Chi Minh forms Vietminh to fight the Japanese.

1945 Japan hands over power to the Vietminh and surrenders to the United States. Ho Chi Minh becomes president of Vietnam. French troops arrive in Vietnam.

1946 War breaks out between France and Vietminh.

1949 Communist victory in China.

1954 France defeated at Dien Bien Phu. Geneva Agreement signed and French troops leave Vietnam.

1955 Ngo Dinh Diem becomes South Vietnamese president and orders the imprisonment of Vietminh suspects.

1957 Vietminh begin guerrilla war in South Vietnam.

1959 First American military advisers killed in Vietnam.

1960 John F. Kennedy elected US president. NLF formed.

1961 Kennedy promises more aid to South Vietnam.

1962 American advisers in Vietnam increased from 700 to 12,000. 'Strategic hamlet' policy begins.

1963 Buddhist protests against Diem begin – Buddhist monks commit suicide by setting fire to themselves. Diem killed in military take-over. President Kennedy assassinated in Dallas. Lyndon Johnson becomes president. 15,000 American advisers in Vietnam.

1964 Congress passes Gulf of Tonkin Resolution. American planes bomb North Vietnam and NLF attack American air bases.

1965 Operation Rolling Thunder begins. First US fighting troops sent to Vietnam, 184,310 US troops in Vietnam.

1966 Johnson resumes bombing of North Vietnam. 385,300 US troops in Vietnam.

1967 Van Thieu becomes South Vietnamese president. 485,600 US troops in Vietnam.

1968 Tet Offensive. Major demonstrations in America against the war. Massacre at My Lai. Johnson announces that he will not stand for re-election. Peace talks begin in Paris. Richard Nixon elected US president. 536,000 US troops in Vietnam.

1969 Nixon begins Vietnamization programme and announces troop withdrawals from Vietnam. Ho Chi Min dies in Hanoi. 484,330 US troops in Vietnam.

1970 In demonstrations at Kent State University, four students killed. 335,790 US troops in Vietnam.

1971 Lieutenant Calley convicted of My Lai massacre. 158,120 US troops in Vietnam.

1972 Nixon re-elected as President. 24,000 US troops in Vietnam.

1973 Cease-fire signed in Paris. Last American troops leave Vietnam.

1974 Nixon resigns over Watergate. Gerald Ford becomes president.

1975 Congress refuses to send American troops to Vietnam. Van Thieu leaves Saigon for Taiwan. Saigon falls to NLF.

Further reading

Books

The Making of Modern America 1948–76, Sally Senzell Isaacs, (History of America), Heinemann Library, 1999

Vietnam, (World Focus) Heinemann Library, 1995

Living Through History, The Twentieth Century World, Nigel Kelly, Rosemary Rees and Jane Shuter, Heinemann Library, 1998

Twentieth Century Perspectives, The Cold War, David Taylor, Heinemann Library, 2001

Journey of 10,000 Miles, Ian Strachen, Methuen, 1997

Sources

Vietnam War, John Simkin, Spartacus, 1987

Vietnam 1939–75, Neil de Marco, Hodder & Stoughton, 1998

Vietnam. Conflict and Change in Indochina, Alan Pollock, Oxford, 1991

Vietnam, the Australian Experience, John Rowe, Time Life, Sydney

Fiction

Onion Tears, Diana Kidd, Viking, 1992

Golden Legends, Ann Ingram, Heinemann, 1998

Vietnam War websites

www.spartacus.schoolnet.co.uk

www.pbs.org/wgbh/amex/vietnam

www.awm.gov.au

Glossary

Agent Orange most common defoliant used in the Vietnam War. It contained dioxin (q.v.) which causes cancer.

amphetamine stimulant which acts on the central nervous system

anti-personnel bombs bombs designed to kill or injure people, e.g. cluster bombs. They contain plastic or steel needles and explode on impact.

ARVN Army of the Republic of Vietnam (South)

blockade to shut off an enemy area, such as a city or port, using troops or ships to stop supplies and messages reaching the enemy

capitalism system which uses private wealth to produce goods

CIA Central Intelligence Agency. This body was responsible for looking after US interests abroad, often by undercover activity.

civil war war between different parties or factions within the same nation

Cold War state of hostility and tension between two countries or power blocs which falls short of open warfare

collective farms large farm or group of small farms organized and run by its workers, usually under communist state control

communist follower of communism – a political system based on the idea that workers and peasants should control the country, its industry and farms. The Soviet Union is widely regarded as the first communist country (following the 1917 revolution).

dioxin chemical which can destroy the brain and central nervous system

domino theory Cold War theory held by many Americans. It proposed that if one country fell to communism then those around it were likely to follow. The theory applies particularly to SE Asia.

draft in the USA, to select for compulsory military service

fragging wounding or killing of officers by their own men

grenade small explosive shell thrown by hand or shot from rifle barrel

guerrilla war type of warfare in which a soldier uses hit-and-run tactics against the enemy which is usually very powerful. A guerrilla soldier will not normally wear a uniform. The word 'guerrilla', Spanish for 'little war', dates from the time between 1807 and 1814 when Spanish soldiers were fighting against Napoleon.

Gulf of Tonkin Resolution US Congress Resolution of 1964 giving the President wide powers to conduct the Vietnam War

herbicide chemicals used to destroy or reduce plant cover. In Vietnam, chemicals were sprayed on the jungle to kill off vegetation so that the Vietcong could not use it for cover.

malaria infectious disease caused by a mosquito bite and characterized by recurring bouts of fever and chills

mangrove tree that grows in muddy swamps or on tropical coasts. The bark is used for tanning and dyeing and the fruit is edible.

napalm jelly-like petrol substance used in incendiary bombs

NLF National Liberation Front

NVA North Vietnamese Army

pacifist one who believes that violence of any kind is unjustifiable and that one should not participate in war

Pentagon US military headquarters near Washington

Pulitzer Prize one of a group of money prizes set up under the will of the American newspaper owner, Joseph Pulitzer. They are awarded annually to Americans for work in music, journalism, history and literature.

re-education process by which thousands of Vietnamese were sent to camps to be instructed in communist theory and obedience to the government

refugees people forced to leave their homes and land, usually because of war

Returned and Services League organization of ex-soldiers who fought in Vietnam

trip-wire wire stretched close to the ground which, when touched, causes an explosion

Vietcong communist-led guerrilla army and political movement

Vietminh organization founded by Ho Chi Minh to fight the French and the Japanese in order to achieve independence.

Index

Titles in the *20th Century Perspectives* series include:

Hardback   0 431 11984 8

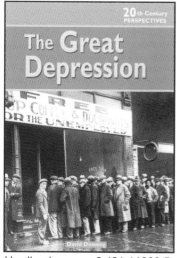

Hardback   0 431 11980 5

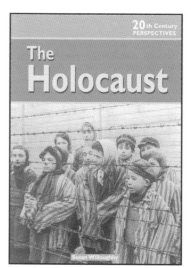

Hardback   0 431 11983 X

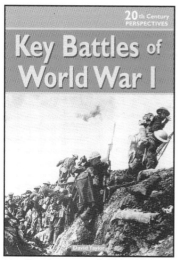

Hardback   0 431 11981 3

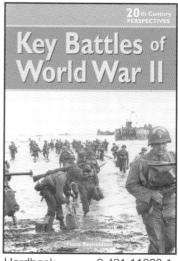

Hardback   0 431 11982 1

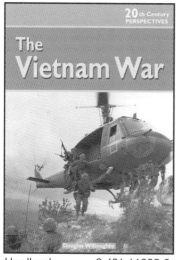

Hardback   0 431 11985 6

Find out about the other titles in this series on our website www.heinemann.co.uk/library